LADY | GAGA

Published by Wise Publications
14-15 Berners Street, London W1T 3LJ, UK.

Exclusive Distributors:
Music Sales Limited
Distriubution Centre, Newmarket Road, Bury St. Edmunds, Suffolk IP33 3YB, UK.
Music Sales Pty Limited
20 Resolution Drive, Caringbah, NSW 2229, Australia.

Order No. AM997920
ISBN 978-1-84938-139-0

Printed in the EU.

www.musicsales.com

JUST DANCE

Words and Music by STEFANI GERMANOTTA,
RedOne and ALIAUNE THIAM

6

8

LOVEGAME

Words and Music by STEFANI GERMANOTTA
and RedOne

13

14

PAPARAZZI

Words and Music by STEFANI GERMANOTTA
and ROB FUSARI

20

POKER FACE

Words and Music by STEFANI GERMANOTTA
and RedOne

Dance Pop

Lyrics:
I wan-na hold 'em like they do in Tex-as plays:
I wan-na roll with him, a hard pair we will be.

EH, EH
(Nothing Else I Can Say)

Words and Music by STEFANI GERMANOTTA
and MARTIN KIERSZENBAUM

BEAUTIFUL, DIRTY, RICH

Words and Music by STEFANI GERMANOTTA
and ROB FUSARI

THE FAME

Words and Music by STEFANI GERMANOTTA
and MARTIN KIERSZENBAUM

42

MONEY HONEY

Words and Music by STEFANI GERMANOTTA,
RedOne and BILAL HAJJI

Moderate Techno groove

That's M - O - N - E - Y, __

__ so sex - y, I. Damn, I love __ the Jag, __ the jet __ and the man-
Damn, I love __ the boat __ by the beach on the west

sion, oh __ yeah. __ And I en - joy __ the gifts __
coast, oh __ yeah. __ And I en - joy __ some fine __

* Recorded a half step higher.

STARSTRUCK

Words and Music by STEFANI GERMANOTTA,
TRAMAR DILLARD, MARTIN KIERSZENBAUM
and NICK DRESTI

Recorded a half step lower.

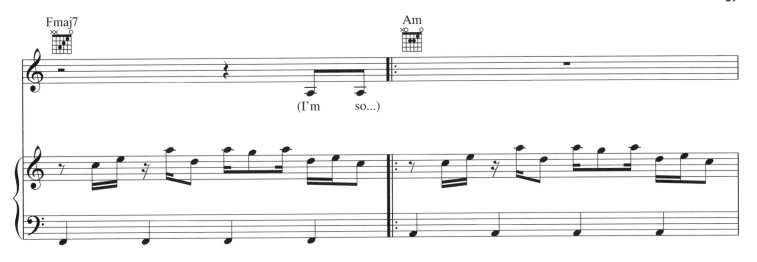

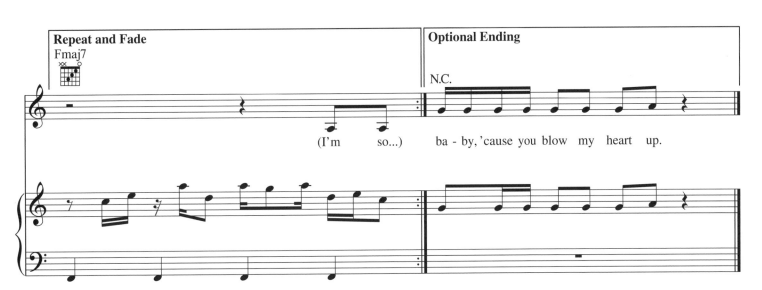

Additional Lyrics

Rap: Hey, lil momma, like really, really, is that him?
I done seen you before. What you got on them big rims?
Enter that cash flow, I'm like, baby, you don't trip.
So shawy, say hand over your signature right here.

Like on just the dotted line, and I'm supposed to sign.
How's she at it? A fanatic, and I think it's goin' down.
She so starstruck, the gal all stuck.
I should have had an overdose, too many Starbucks.

Ain't never seen a balla, paper that stack taller.
Notice who let the top back on the Chevy Impala.
Hummers and all that fully loaded with two spoilers.
What did you call that when you showed up with two dollars?

But that's another chapter, son of a bachelor.
All one me, just spotted baby actor.
Complete swagga, there go the dagger.
Got what she wants, shawty happily ever after.

BOYS BOYS BOYS

Words and Music by STEFANI GERMANOTTA
and RedOne

Dance tempo

Hey there, sug-ar ba-by, saw you twice at the pop __ show.
Ba-by is a bad boy with some ret-ro __ sneak-ers.

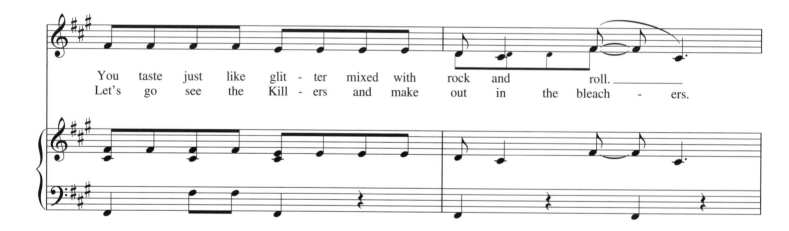

You taste just like glit-ter mixed with rock and roll. __
Let's go see the Kill-ers and make out in the bleach-ers.

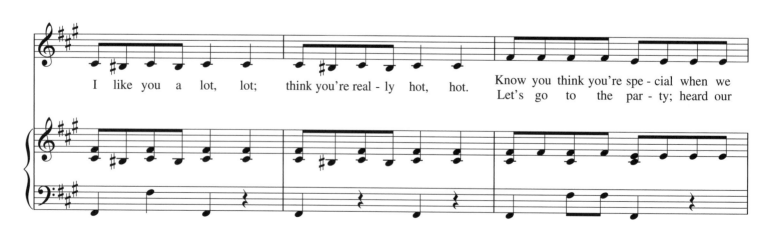

I like you a lot, lot; think you're real-ly hot, hot. Know you think you're spe-cial when we
Let's go to the par-ty; heard our

PAPER GANGSTA

Words and Music by STEFANI GERMANOTTA
and RedOne

Moderately

Mid - night __ rush with a pen in my hand; __ ink-
Got __ some - thing real - ly shin - y to start; __ want

in' Lin - coln, sand - script with a fan. __ Re -
me to sign there on your Range Rov - er heart? __ I've

mem - ber - ing __ me be - fore it be - gan; __ some - times I felt so Def in the Jam. __ But the
heard it be - fore; yeah, the din - ners were nice, __ till your dia - mond words melt - ed in - to some ice. __ You __

*Recorded a half step lower.

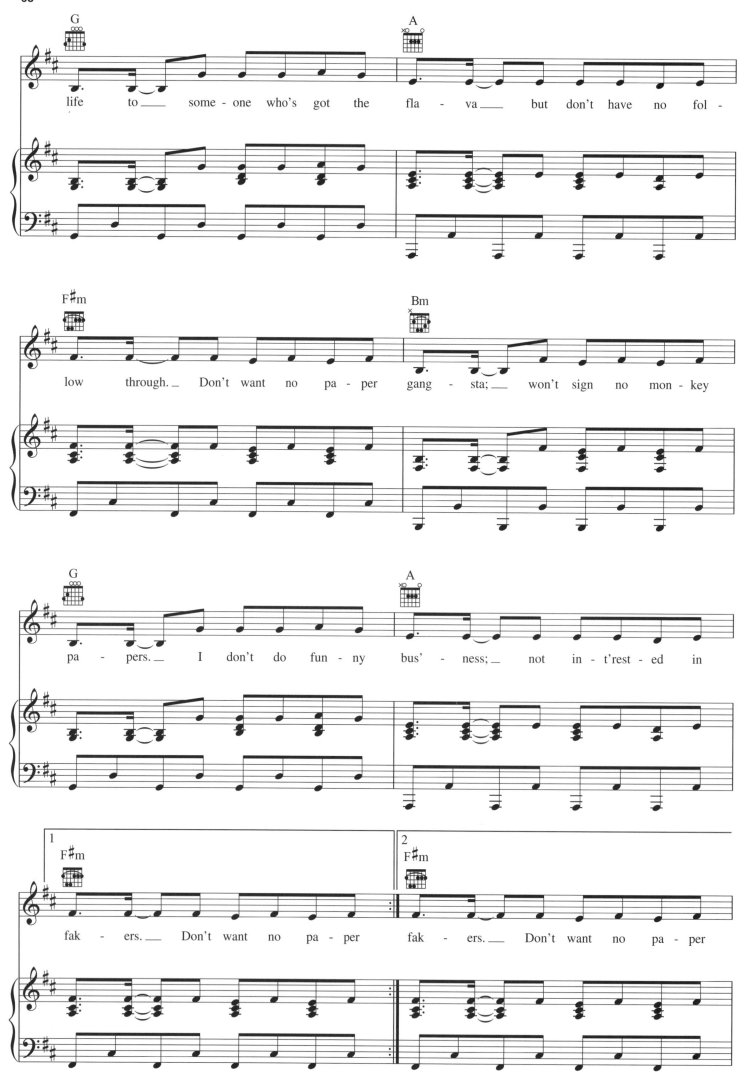

BROWN EYES

Words and Music by STEFANI GERMANOTTA
and ROB FUSARI

I LIKE IT ROUGH

Words and Music by STEFANI GERMANOTTA
and MARTIN KIERSZENBAUM

76

SUMMERBOY

Words and Music by STEFANI GERMANOTTA,
BRIAN KIERULF and JOSHUA SCHWARTZ